ITALIAN

ART DECO

STEVEN HELLER

I T A

GRAPHIC DESIGN

A R T

CHRONICLE BOOKS

& L O U I S E F I L I

L I A N

B E T W E E N T H E W A R S

D E C O

S A N F R A N C I S C O

Words cannot express our appreciation to Sonia Biancalani Levethan, our researcher, who worked as sleuth, liaison, and transla-tor. Thanks to Nion McEvoy, our editor; Michael Carabetta, art director; and Charlotte Stone, assistant editor, at Chronicle Books for their encouragement and guidance. Thanks also to Lee Bearson at Louise Fili Ltd. for his design and computer exper-tise. And Sarah Jane Freymann, our agent.

This book would not have been possible had it not been for the cooperation and generosity of scholars and collectors in the United States and Italy. The following were especially helpful in locating and providing us with materials and sharing invaluable leads: Mitchell Wolfson, Peggy Lore, and Anita Gross of the Wolfsonian Foundation, Miami, Florida; Kathy Leff, editor of the *Journal of Decorative and Propaganda Arts*; Michael Sheehe and Elaine Lustig Cohen of Ex Libris, New York; Bob Brown of Reinhold Brown Gallery, New York; George Theofiles of Miscellaneous Man, New Freedom, Pennsylvania; Jack Banning of Poster America, New York; Dr. James Fraser of the Library at Fairleigh Dickinson University, Madison, New Jersey; Luigi and Paolo Lazzaroni of Lazzaroni & C.S.p.A., Saronno; Geom. Egidio Bossetti of Davide Campari Milano S.p.A., Milan; Sergio Coradeschi, Milan; Anna Maria Gandini of Milano Libri, Milan; Prof. Eugenio Manzato, Museo Civico L. Bailo, Treviso; Francoa Arduini, Director Biblioteca Marucelliana, Florence; Enrico Castruccio, Milan; Peter Weiss, Munich; Leo Lionni, Radda in Chianti; Gloria Bianchino, Director Centro Studie Archivio della Comunicazione dell' Università degli Studi di Parma; Cecilia Giudici Servetti, Librarian, Biblioteca dei Musei Civici Torino; the staff of Museo Civico di Treviso; Giuseppina Chiesa, Director Chiesa Rotograf, s.r.l. Tavagnacco, Udine; Anthony Pizzuto, Librarian, and Chris McKee, Head Librarian, New York Public Library Periodical Division, New York; Louise Porter, Librarian, Boston Public Library, Boston. Thanks also to Giovanni Salviati and Matteo Tresoldi, Milan, for additional photography.

We were also guided to and through public archives, private collections, bookstores, and flea markets by our friends Paolo Guidotti, Lita Talarico, Paola Antonelli, Greg Leeds, and Lucia Perucci.

Finally, thanks to Steven Guarnaccia for jump-starting our research by allowing us to borrow from his extensive (and eclectic) collection.—SH & LF

Research assistance by Sonia Biancalani Levethan. Art direction: Louise Fili. Design: Louise Fili and Lee Bearson. Display typeface design by Jonathan Hoeffler.

Italy's applied graphic art of the twenties and thirties was exemplary in Europe for its persuasive power. A synthesis of avant garde and vernacular styles reflecting the political and cultural revolutions of the age, Italian graphic style was at once raucous and elegant. While it rejected a great artistic heritage, its roots dug deep into the past.

The *Risorgimento*, or second Italian renaissance, climaxed in 1861 when King Victor Emmanuel II, with the help of guerrilla leader Giuseppe Garibaldi, conquered and unified most of the Italian peninsula's independent city states. But even as Rome was not built in a day, Italy did not mature into statehood overnight. The trappings of nationalism developed slowly, as did an Italian graphic style, which, despite Italy's legacy as the cradle of European humanist art, took shape as a melange of foreign influences until the early twentieth century, when a national identity was forged out of modern art.

Italy's typographic heritage (the Roman letter, the model for the Western world's most significant typefaces, was originally derived from carved inscriptions on the Trajan column, A.D. 114) exerted little obvious influence on the direction of Italian graphic art and design during the late nineteenth century. Rather than build upon the classicism of fifteenth-century Venetian printers or the elegance of the eighteenth-century typographer Giambattista Bodoni, whose *Manuale Tipografico* (1788) was a guide to modern letterforms, Italian typographers and graphic artists turned their attention to French trends, like Post-Impressionism and Art Nouveau. The latter was known in Italy as Stile Liberty, and by the turn of the century this "floreated madness" had pervaded Italian design and architecture.

By the early twentieth century Milan was a crossroads of culture, commerce, and industry. Graphic artists from all over Europe traveled and worked there. Likewise, Italian artists visited the capitals of European modern art — Paris, Berlin, and Vienna — and carried home the Belle Epoch's most emblematic posters and periodicals. Europe's premier art, culture, and satire journals such as Munich's *Jugend* and *Simplicisimus* and London's *Studio* influenced a shift in Italian advertising art from nineteenth-century romantic illustration to twentieth-century objective imagery. These styles also were embraced in response to Italy's late change from an agrarian (and craft-oriented) economy to an industrial one, precipitating the development of commercial markets in Italy and abroad. Around 1900 "the first posters completely designed and composed by Italian artists appeared in Italy," wrote N. G. Fiumi, a critic for the English magazine *Commercial Art*. "It is, therefore, not [inappropriate] to say that Italy was one of the last important countries to make use of artistic advertisements." Italy's graphic artists borrowed visual languages as an expedient way to promote Italian products. Yet mimicking European styles was also a step toward developing an indigenous Italian one.

Among the progenitors of modern Italian graphic identity, Leopoldo Metlicovitz (1868–1944) and Adolfo Hohenstein (1854–unknown), both foreign

FIERA DI TRIPOLI
Advertising stamp for fair
1936

born Italians, became masters of the "new manifesti" with styles that drew upon lyrical heroism and organic decoration. As skilled realists they turned the common-place into allegories: an automobile poster did not show a car but personified speed; a department store ad did not show a garment but celebrated universal beauty. Although their personal styles developed away from French Art Nouveau, they were nevertheless rooted in the aesthetics of the Belle Epoch. Conversely, one of Italy's early modern innovators, Leonetto Cappiello (1875–1942), assimilated his European influences (i.e., Cheret and Lautrec) so well that he might be consid-ered *the* pioneer of an Italian style. Born in Livorno, Cappiello lived and worked in Paris where he mastered the revolutionary concepts of space and dynamic composi-tion being introduced into French painting. An acerbic caricaturist, he manipulated comic figures that embodied the ideals or essence of a product. Equally influential was Marcello Dudovich (1878–1962) who, though born in Trieste, spent most of his working life in Milan where he practiced a type of Art Nouveau that combined exquisite draftsmanship with elegant styling. His posters of men and women in monumental poses bolstered the identities of such major Italian businesses as La Rinascente department store, Pirelli tires, and Borsalino hats. Another graphic artist of the twenties to contribute to the Italian identity, Marcello Nizzoli (1887–1967), was known for his classically inspired posters for Campari and others. About Nizzoli, N.G. Fuimi commented in *Commercial Art*, "I believe that the rea-sons for his success are to be found in the fact that he does not borrow from his contemporaries, but seeks all his inspiration from our great artists of the past, interpreting their aims with modern feeling."

This could be said about many of the leading names in Italian graphic art who reconciled their heritage with the modern. Not all Italian artists, however, were so responsive to their times. The movement known as "Novecento," which began after World War I under the influence of poet and would-be dictator Gabriele D'Annunzio (1863–1938), recalled the grandeur of ancient Rome in literature, painting, graphic art, and architecture. Novecento attempted to mythologize Italian history, and its exponents did succeed in creating a distinctly Italian design style by falsifying tradition. The result was pretentious art. Although Italian commercial art of the teens and early twenties was dominated by Stile Liberty and later Novecento, inventive practitioners tried the contemporary styles being unveiled throughout post-war Europe. The new graphic style known as Art Moderne (or Art Deco, a term coined in the sixties as a contraction of the 1925 Exposition Internationale des Arts Décoratifs et Industriels Modernes in Paris), is referred to by historian Bevis Hillier as "the last of the total styles." A broad-based aesthetic, Art Deco was a synthesis of ancient Greek, Egyptian, and Mayan decorative motifs, Cubist painting, and Machine Age symbols. After 1925 it became the dominant design trend in virtually all the industrialized nations as applied to a wide range of products and forms.

The Italian hybrid of Art Deco graphic design was the offspring of two

CATTOLICA
LA SPIAGGIA INTER-
NAZIONALE DELL'
ADRIATICO
Advertisement for
vacation resort, 1933
Erberto Carboni

CROCIERA AEREA
TRANSATLANTICA
ITALIA - BRASILE
Poster for airline, 1930

volatile parents: Futurism and Fascism — with consumerism serving as its stabilizing grandparent. Futurism, one of the twentieth century's earliest avant garde art movements, was founded in 1909 by F.T. Marinetti, a writer, poet, and painter, whose self-professed mission was to "challenge inertia" through perpetual disruption of the status quo. In poetry this meant replacing conventional verse with explosive rhythms and rhymes (in what he called *parole in liberta* or "words in freedom") that mimicked the sound of machines and weapons. In art this required destroying traditional notions of space and composition in order to express the dynamism of technology. And in typography this resulted in obliterating any semblance of classical symmetry on the printed page. "I am beginning a typographical revolution," wrote Marinetti in one of the movement's many hyperbolic manifestos. "My revolution is against the so called 'typographic harmony of the page,' which stands in direct opposition to the changes of style, moods, etc., which are typical of the style in which the page has been written. That is why we will use three or four different ink colors in the same page, and up to twenty different typefaces when needed." Many of the typefaces used were drawn from seventeenth-century specimen sheets, indicating that even the revolution in design could not be effected overnight.

Like the Futurists, the Italian Fascists were dedicated to violently attacking the ruling monarchy and bourgeoisie who, in the wake of World War I, were accused by nationalists of having sold out the nation to foreign powers. Both groups — Futurist and Fascist — were committed to social revolution and *Italianismo.* While Marinetti used art (often in concert with bombastic demonstrations) to propagate his vision, Benito Mussolini, a former socialist who switched allegiances to lead the Fascist party, used brute force in terrorizing his opponents. Though not always in agreement, Futurist and Fascist movements literally marched to the same drum in 1919 when they fought in the *Fasco di combattenti,* illegal paramilitary bands who fomented unrest.

The Fascist revolution succeeded without bloodshed when, in 1922, King Victor Emmanuel II succumbed to the threat of a Fascist march on Rome and invited Mussolini to become premier. Many Italians initially viewed Fascism as a first step towards ousting "old mummies and rotten figures," and so youthful Futurists threw their support behind the new regime by publicizing it in their periodicals, posters, and books. Marinetti held advertising in high regard, and saw its conventions as an effective way to propagate the Futurist faith, hence much of Futurism's early propaganda was presented in traditional formats. "Marinetti understood the power of advertising," wrote a critic, "which must reach people at every depth and height, excluding nobody from the social landscape." Futurists, however, took a more radical step: rather than products they sold ideas — an unprecedented use of advertising that required unprecedented approaches. Soon the Futurists began playing with graphic form. The results were anarchic compositions and symbolic letterforms.

GIORNATA DELL'ALA
Postcard for air show, 1931
Ver

Advertising techniques were adopted for use in other European avant garde movements during the 1920s. Dutch De Stijl, German Bauhaus and Dada, and Russian Constructivism all followed Marinetti's lead. All published self-promotional literature, designed books, and subsequently influenced radical changes in mainstream design practices. Nevertheless, these movements were kept out of the mainstream. The Constructivists played a role in the Soviet propaganda machine until they were superseded in the late 1920s by Stalin's Socialist Realism. The Futurists were favored as long as they concentrated on Mussolini's key objective, the creation of a Fascist image, but their vehement attacks on Italian traditions made them a thorn in the side of most Fascists, many of whom preferred Novecento. One member of the ruling council attacked them as "nothing but a group of poor little students [who] ran away from Jesuit school, who made some noise in the nearby woods and then had to be brought back home by [their] guardian."

Despite the Futurists' devotion to industry, they were held in contempt by industrialists. With few exceptions, most Futurist advertising was used either as self-promotion or by adventuresome companies. "It is easy to imagine how the Futurists, considering themselves as the first and most audacious apologists of industrial society, must have encountered a certain frustration . . . for not having been fully used by the fields of applied arts and industry," wrote Claudia Salaris in *Il Futurismo e la Pubblicità* (Luptetti & Co., 1988). Indeed it was a struggle to convince business that these unprecedented approaches were advantageous. One

**TRIENNALE
D'OLTREMARE**
Poster for nationalist
celebration, c. 1940
Cella

supporter of Futurist design wrote about the need to influence Italian business this way: "It is necessary to force the industrialists to understand that a good poster and a good concept [must] generate . . . from the very modern brain of new men — everyone of them full of the dynamic and fast mechanism of our time, and capable of the most daring experiments of color and design." In the end, certain Futurist aesthetics were imitated by non-Futurist designers.

Image was the heart of Fascist politics, and graphic design was its backbone. Mussolini often became an art director when in detailed memoranda he criticized subordinates for their poor use of type or the placement of banners and posters. Yet in the early years of his regime he allowed artists leeway in the development of a Fascist style — hence the coexistence of Futuristic, Art Moderne, and Novecento approaches in art and architecture. "We must not take advantage of our heritage from the past," wrote Mussolini. "We must create a new heritage to be connected to the old one, creating a new art, an art of our times, a Fascist art." Ultimately, however, compromise came, at the expense of the avant garde when the dynamic aspects of Futurism were incorporated into an Italian Art Deco.

For a regime that promoted a cult of youth, the streamlined — or futuristic — aspects of Art Deco were the perfect vehicle for mythic depiction, and the airbrush was the best tool for achieving blemish-free effects. Art Deco expressed romanticism in its smooth surfaces and monumentalism in its rectilinear forms. Deco depictions of Fascist blackshirts made thugs look snappy and stylish. Even

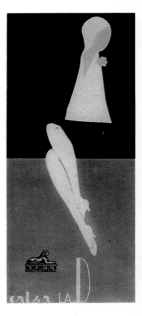

CALZA LA D
Poster for stockings, 1932

the *faces*, the charged emblem of the Fascist regime taken from ancient Roman iconography, was often streamlined through Art Deco conceit to symbolize the futuristic ideals of the party.

Italian Art Deco was not only manifest in political imagery but was propagated through design and printing trade journals and exhibitions aimed at designers working for industry and commerce. In the late twenties the Futurists did their best to influence these designers through manifestos like "Futurism and Advertising" (1932), by Fortunato Depero (1892–1960), Futurism's most dedicated advertising designer, who asserted that "the art of the future will be mainly advertising." Ambitious exhibitions of publicity were common; at the 1928 Futurist Festival, Enrico Prampolini designed an advertising pavilion. Other periodicals used to propagate modernity included Milan's *L'Ufficio Moderno – La Pubblicità*, which critiqued the latest design trends. *Graphicus*, published in Turin at the same time, was moderately progressive in its attempts to reconcile the Modern and modernistic. Beginning in 1937 the Fascist Syndicate for Advertising published *La Pubblicità d'Italia*, which set standards that indicated a preference for the modernistic over the Modern, but gradually programmed a stylistic shift toward Fascist realism. In contrast to official Fascist preferences, *Campo Grafico*, a decidedly progressive technical review, started in 1933, was rooted in Bauhaus principles and proffered a distinctly rationalist method (marking the ascendancy of the graphic designer over the painter) that became dominant after World War II.

Campo Grafico promoted a canon of composition consistent with the New Typography and "a mechanical art for a mechanical age" (i.e., photographs should replace painting), but action was taken by only a few intrepid designers, most notably in the layouts of the architecture magazine *Casabella*, or practiced by the members of Milan's Studio Boggeri. By the mid-thirties, mainstream Italian graphic design was ostensibly modernistic; it remained image-oriented and display types influenced by Futurism were common, including hand-drawn letterforms that accentuated the improvisational.

The evolution of Italian Art Deco from Futurism and Art Moderne took a decade or so to achieve, reaching its peak around 1939 when the demands of Mussolini's imperialism and the looming war forced a shift in design policy to decidedly unambiguous propaganda. Art Deco, perfect in peacetime for lulling Italians into a false security, and into accepting Fascism as a benevolent regime, was inappropriate when Mussolini demanded sacrifice and discipline.

From the beginning the Nazis forced all German artists to conform to rigid National Socialist standards, while the Fascists tolerated design pluralism as long as the symbols of the regime were not violated. What distinguishes Italian graphic design between the wars from other totalitarian countries was a modicum of individuality. In the final analysis, Italian Art Deco — futuristic and raucous, classic and monumental, humorous and hyperbolic — represented the spirit of the era, and all its contradictions.

FIERA DI VIENNA
Advertising stamp for fair
1936

**PROPAGANDA
ANTITUBERCOLARE**
Poster for tuberculosis
prevention, c. 1934
Latin

The radical agendas of Constructivism and the Bauhaus caused Stalin to end one and Hitler to close the other. Mussolini did not suppress the Futurists but reconciled the needs of his regime with their value as visual propagandists able to synthesize the avant garde and modernistic. In 1923 he wrote, "I don't want to encourage anything that can be similar to an 'Art of the State.'" Nevertheless he understood that a Fascist identity combining classicism and modernism would appeal to old and young; especially the youths at whom Fascist mythology was directed. Mussolini wanted a Fascist image that reflected Roman glory yet symbolized the future. "He grasped intuitively that an image is built from the bottom up," writes historian Gian Poalo Ceserani, "by what happens on a day-to-day basis — with the road signs, the buildings, and emblems." In 1921 thirty percent of all Italians were illiterate, and graphic images were the most effective way of addressing them. Mussolini saw Italians as "political consumers," and as Fascism's "creative director" he controlled their behavior through slogans and symbols.

IL LIBRO DELLA IIᴬ CLASSE
Textbook cover, 1932
Mario Pompei

QUADERNO
Notebook cover, c. 1939
A. Rigorini

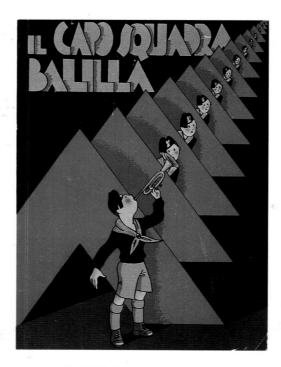

IL CAPO SQUADRA BALILLA
Cover for Fascist youth handbook, 1935
Zedda

STORIA E GEOGRAFIA
Textbook cover, 1933

LETTURE CLASSE SECONDA
Textbook cover, 1932
Angelo Della Torre

MACEDONIA
Cigarette advertisement,
c. 1935

GIOVENTÙ FASCISTA
Magazine cover, 1932

GIOVENTÙ FASCISTA
Magazine cover, 1931
Cesare Gobbo

GIOVENTÙ FASCISTA
Magazine cover, 1932

GIOVENTÙ FASCISTA
Magazine cover, 1931
Cesare Gobbo

ANNO X OND
Poster for athletic
competition, 1932
G. Pessani

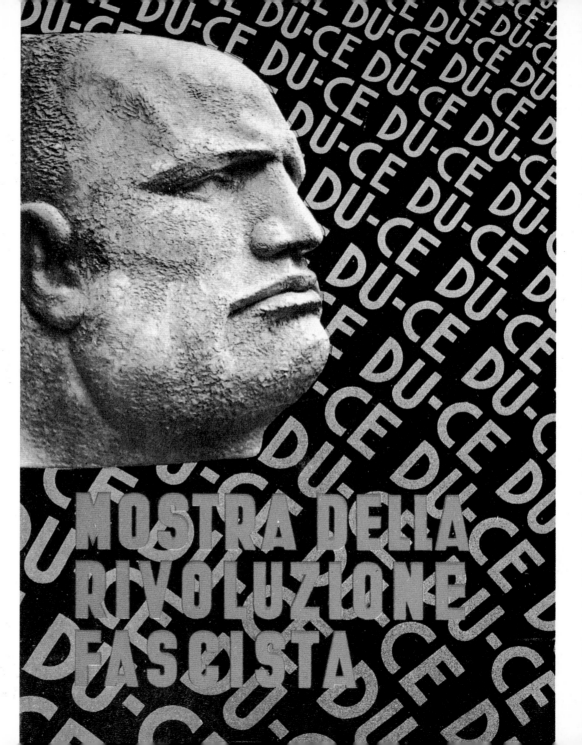

24

BONIFICA INTEGRALE
Book illustration, 1932
A. Calzavara

CONTRO LA TUBERCOLOSI
Diploma, c. 1938
Giuseppe Latini

OPERA BALILLA
Report card, 1944

**RICOSTRUZIONI
ZONE DI GUERRA**
Book illustration, 1933
A. Calzavara

**MOSTRA DELLA
RIVOLUZIONE FASCISTA**
Exhibition poster, 1933
C.V. Testi

MOSTRA NAZIONALE DEL GRANO
Exhibition poster, 1932
Marcello Nizzoli

Italian culture between the wars was not rooted in the artistic heritage of humanist art and architecture from the Renaissance, but developed out of twentieth-century rebellion. Throughout Europe modernist vanguards were attacking archaic political, social, and cultural institutions. No movement was more fervent than the Italian Futurists and their attacks on timeworn ideas. Speed symbolized progress; and the engine became the icon of rebirth. The Futurists devised new images and graphic forms to represent a cultural vision that was inextricably wed to their social one. Marinetti believed in "life as art," the total integration of day-to-day reality and the creative process. Hierarchies imposed by the old cultural elite, targeted for destruction, were to be replaced by social equality: "To communicate [efficiently] it is necessary to talk to the masses, not just the individual." This maxim, promoted in the "Futurist Reconstruction of the Universe" (1932) was perpetuated in periodicals. Yet despite their sincere attempts, what the Futurists called mass art was not necessarily consistent with what the masses needed or wanted.

**NUOVO TEATRO
FUTURISTA**
Theater poster, 1924
Fortunato Depero

**MARINETTI: PAROLE
IN LIBERTÀ FUTURISTE**
Book cover and inside pages, 1932
Tulia D'Albisola

TULIO D'ALBISOLA
Book cover and inside pages, 1934
Bruno Munari

DA I NUOVI POETI FUTURISTI
Typographic page, 1925
F.T. Marinetti

MARINETTI: VULCANI
Book cover, 1927
Enrico Prampolini

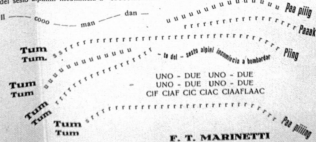

Corvée d'acqua sotto i forti Austriaci.

STILE FUTURISTA
Magazine cover, 1934
V. Pozzo

DIZIONARIO AEREO
Book jacket, 1925

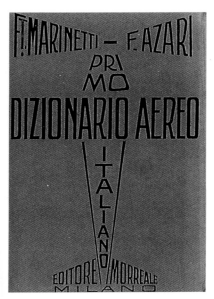

SCATOLE D'AMORE
BY F.T. MARINETTI
Book cover, c. 1932
Ivo Pannagi

NOI #1
Magazine cover, 1923
Enrico Prampolini

FUTURISMO
Newspaper front page, 1933

MODERNISSIMA
Catalog cover, 1920
Marcello Nizzoli

ASSOC. UNIVERSITARIA PARMENSE
Calendar, 1926
Erberto Carboni

IL MIO & IL TUO
Sheet music, 1930
Bonfanti

1931
Calendar
G. Acquaviva

ALMANACCO ITALIANO
Almanac cover, 1934

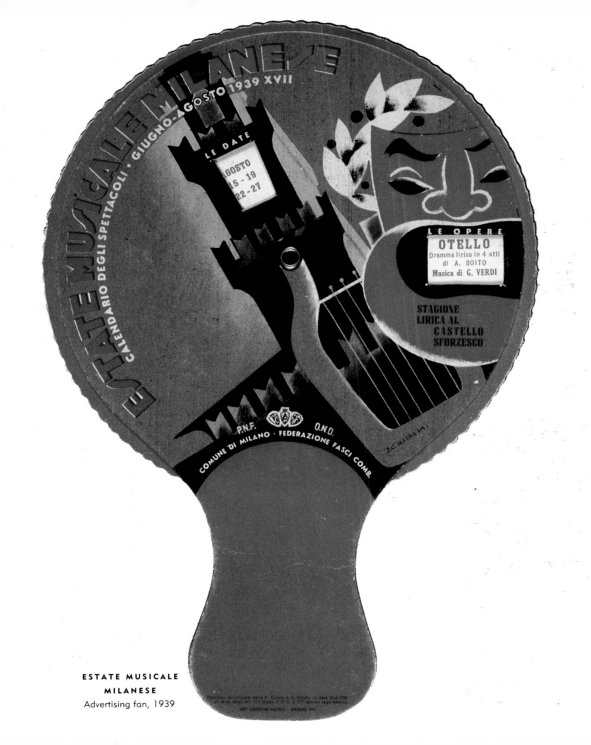

**ESTATE MUSICALE
MILANESE**
Advertising fan, 1939

BERTELLI
Calendar, 1937
F. Romoli

GLOMERULI O GOCCE RUGGERI
Calendar, 1935
G. Guillermaz

BERTELLI
Calendar, 1932

BERTELLI
Calendar, 1936

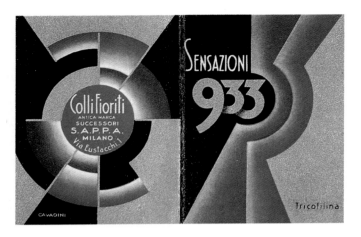

COLLI FIORITI
Calendar, 1933
Alfredo Cavadini

OPSO PARMA
Calendar, 1932
Erberto Carboni

BERTELLI
Calendar, 1939
F. Romoli

TENDENZE SPORTIVE
Calendar, 1935

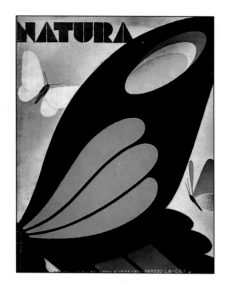

NATURA
Magazine cover, 1932
Paolo Garretto

**IL GIORNALINO
DELLA DOMENICA**
Magazine cover, 1929
B. Ottonelli

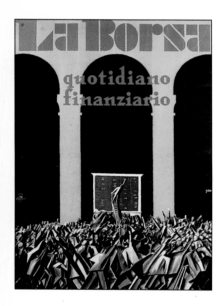

LA BORSA
Magazine cover, 1936
Mario Sironi

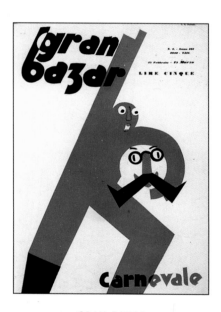

GRAN BAZAR
Magazine cover, 1930
Lucio Venna

EMPORIUM
Magazine cover, 1929
Santam Brogio

LA RIVISTA
Magazine cover, 1933
Fortunato Depero

SECOLO XX
Magazine cover, 1928
Tio

EMPORIUM
Magazine cover, 1928

LA RIVISTA
Magazine cover, 1939
Paolo Garretto

SEGNILIBRI
Bookmarks, 1930s

LA CITTÀ DI ABACO
Children's book (front and back cover), 1928
Antonio Rubino

L'ARCO DEI SETTE COLORI
Children's book (front and back cover), 1928
Antonio Rubino

Futurist fashion designers produced garments and textiles with outrageous graphics, such as Fortunato Depero's vest (page 44), but their influence on mass-market fashion was minor. Italy had a long tradition of shoe and headwear manufacturing, and some of the country's finest artists were employed to promote these products. Nevertheless, a graphic revolution in the field of fashion advertising occurred in the late twenties with a shift from what historian Giuseppe Priarone refers to as "idea-characters," the metaphoric mascots pioneered by Leonetto Cappiello, to the "idea-goal" devised by Sepo (neé Severo Pozzati, 1895-1983). The concept is here represented by Sepo's poster for Tortonese (page 45), a clothing manufacturer (originally called La Merveilleuse but forced to change its name owing to a law prohibiting Italian business from having foreign-sounding names). Sepo created a unique fashion symbol by overlapping a female figure with a mannequin, whose shape is formed by a ribbon. The poster reveals the confluence of Art Moderne styling and Cubist composition common to much Italian graphic design.

BIANCO
Department store
advertisement, 1926
Sepo

PARANASS

IL SOPRABITO IMPERMEABILE PER TUTTI I TEMPI

PARANASS
Raincoat label, 1931

BORRI
Shoe label, 1928

MALÚ
Clothes label, 1938

PANICOTTO FUTURISTA
Vest, 1923-4
Fortunato Depero

CLAUDIO
Clothes label, 1941

TORTONESE
Poster for clothing store, 1934
Sepo

IVOREA
Rayon label, 1933

QUINTÈ
Label for shoes, c. 1930

RIVELLA
Advertisement for furs, 1932
Erberto Carboni

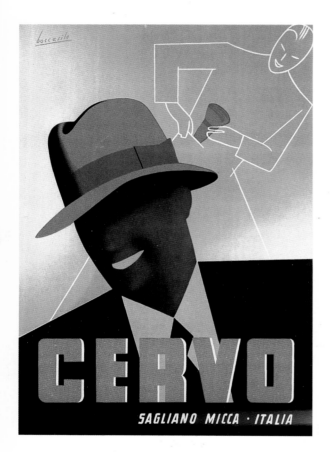

CERVO
Poster for rainhat, 1935
Gino Boccasile

BORSALINO
Poster for hats, c. 1938

ALFIERI & LACROIX S. A. - MILANO

LORD
Poster for hats, 1930
Paolo Garretto

LORD

GOLF
Clothes logo, 1931

AMARO GAMBAROTTA
Advertisement for tuxedo, 1928
Saxida

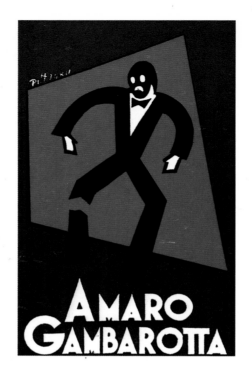

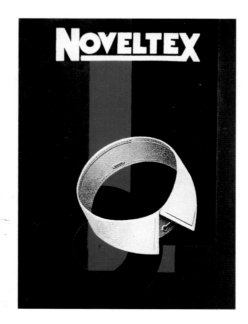

ADORNIA
Button manufacturer logo, 1934
Enrico Stern

NOVELTEX
Poster for shirt collars, 1930
Sepo

SAIRA
Advertisement for fabric, 1936

REM
Poster for clothes, c. 1935
A. Berretti

LUIGI BIANCHI
Clothes logo, 1941

PAOLO ZALVIN
Clothes logo, 1929

Graphics for industry during the twenties and thirties were at once sophisticated and naive. Should technology be given a human face, or should the machine be glorified on its own terms? Within the Futurist ranks there was no question that the machine was sacred. But Futurism was not embraced by many Italian businesses. Company trademarks reveal a certain timidity — graphic puns and anthropomorphized or comic figures were used to individualize what critics called the depersonalization of mass production. The earliest industrial images were similar to those used to depict agriculture; industry was characterized as a muscular hero expending great energy to accomplish the task at hand. Eventually the machine and factory were celebrated for their own inherent virtues. And soon the robot — as used in Futurist advertising — became a comic, and therefore friendly, personification of industrial achievement. That Italy was unequivocally industrialized by the late twenties was demonstrated graphically by the increased number of manufacturing motifs used in everyday advertising and design.

RADIO PERFECTA
Radio logo, 1928

A. PALMIERI
Paint logo, 1932

TUBITOGNI
Pipe logo, 1929

SOCIETÀ ANONIMA CURTI
Factory logo, 1930

ASTRALUX
Lamp logo, 1934
Emilio Zava

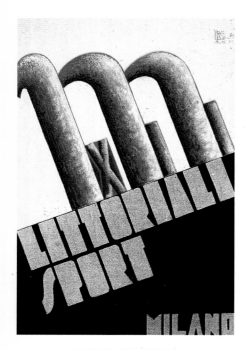

LITTORIALI SPORT
Postcard for sports fair, 1934
Latis

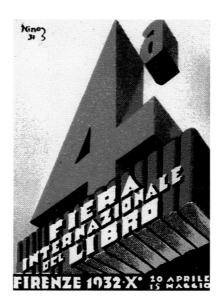

**4^ FIERA INTERNAZIONALE
DEL LIBRO**
Poster stamp for book fair, 1931
Ninoz

XII FIERA DI PADOVA
Poster stamp for city fair 1930
Lucio Venna

CAMPIONATI MONDIALI DI CALCIO
Poster for soccer game, 1934
Mario Gros

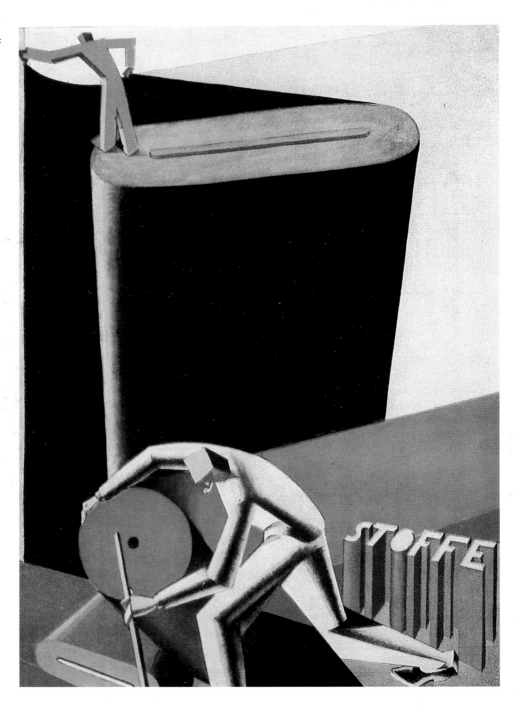

MATA
Insecticide logo, c. 1943

ALBERTO ZANLARI
Postcard for printer, 1930
Erberto Carboni

TAPPETI DI LINOLEUM
Advertisement for linoleum, 1940
Giaci Mondaini

PICATOR
Insecticide logo, 1933

**MOSTRA INTERNAZIONALE
DELLE INDUSTRIE DEL CUOIO**
Poster stamp for exhibition, 1931
Marcello Nizzoli

**FIERA NAZIONALE
DELL' ARTIGIANATO**
Postcard for fair, 1937
Giovanni Cappelli

ESTATE FRIULANA
Poster for festival, 1935
U. Grignaschi

VIᵃ MOSTRA MERCATO
Postcard for fair, 1936
Giuseppe Riccobaldi

SCREMIN
Postcard for furniture company, 1929
Tonelli

GNUDI
Poster stamp for furniture
manufacturer, 1924
Atla

CANTÙ ALLA FIERA DI MILANO
Postcard for fair, 1934

LUBRIFICANTI FIAT
Advertisement for motor oil, 1930
Marcello Nizzoli

DA LEONARDO A MARCONI
Textbook cover, 1932

MOSTRA DELLA LUCE
Postcard for exhibition, 1933
Virgilio Retrosi

Making art reflect aspects of everyday life was not as revolutionary as the Futurists might have thought, for around the turn of the century many producers of sundries, cosmetics, and other quotidian products used modern conceits in their package designs. By the mid-twenties Art Moderne was applied to a variety of beauty and hygenic products, such as perfumes, talcs, bath oils, soaps, and toothpastes — even medicines. Though influenced by trends in modern art these stylish labels and packages, well suited to graphics that symbolize luxury and leisure, resulted primarily from competition on the shelves and racks of the *farmacias*. Store windows offered exuberent displays of Art Deco graphics. Cigarettes were also swathed in appealing imagery. Since Italians consumed them like candy, cigarettes were often packaged and promoted like confections, using motifs that suggested both adventure and chic. Delightful product graphics were applied to stationery and writing implements as well. Imaginatively designed pen-nib and pencil boxes brightened up the shelves and diverted the consumer's eye.

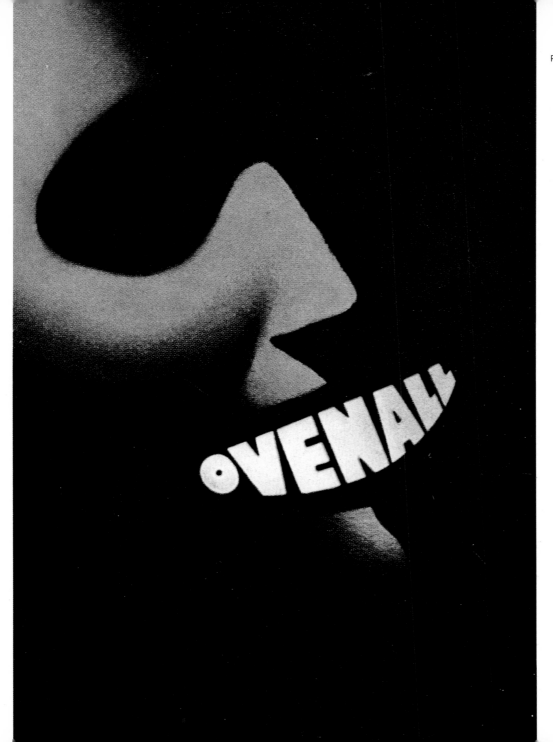

OVENALL
Poster for toothpaste, 1942
Zoltan Tamasi

CANTELE
Bath oil label, 1929

BERTONI
Package for toothpaste, 1933

KOLAPEPTIDE
Advertisement for tonic, 1937

TERGOL
Feminine hygiene product, 1929

FIORELLINI
Talc label, c. 1940

CIPRIA DORIA
Powder label, c. 1935

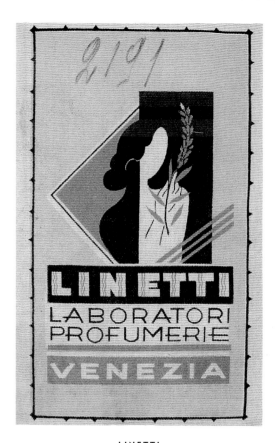

LINETTI
Perfume package, c. 1935

CARLO TACCHINI
Shaving cream label, 1928

S. A. ANTONIO
Tonic label, 1934

BEBÉ
· Soap label, 1944

PETALIA
Powder package, 1928

OSSIGENAL
Bath oil label, 1937

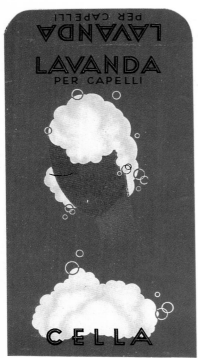

CELLA
Shampoo label, 1934

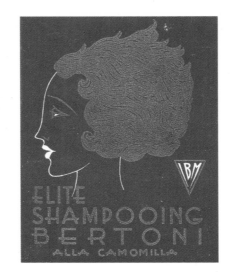

BERTONI
Shampoo label, 1935

LILIA
Powder label, 1935

CIPRIA NOTTON
Powder package, 1935

NUOVO FIORE
Soap label, 1936

MERYBELL
Perfume label, 1936

PROFUMI
Various perfume labels, c. 1930

TOSI
Perfume label, 1924

SOLE
Soap label, 1937

GISBERTO VALLAGUZZA
Powder label, c. 1934

RUDY
Lipstick label, 1937

VICTORIA
Hair perms logo, 1938

MARGOT
Cosmetics label, c. 1930

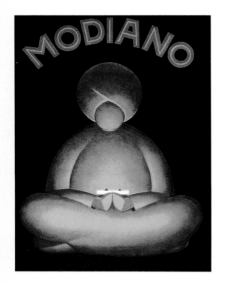

MODIANO
Poster for cigarettes, 1930
Federico Seneca

TIM
Cigarette logo, 1937

MATOSSIAN
Advertisement for cigarettes, 1931
Erberto Carboni

RÉGIE FRANÇAISE
Poster for cigarettes, 1928
Sepo

ROMA
Advertisement for cigarettes, c. 1931

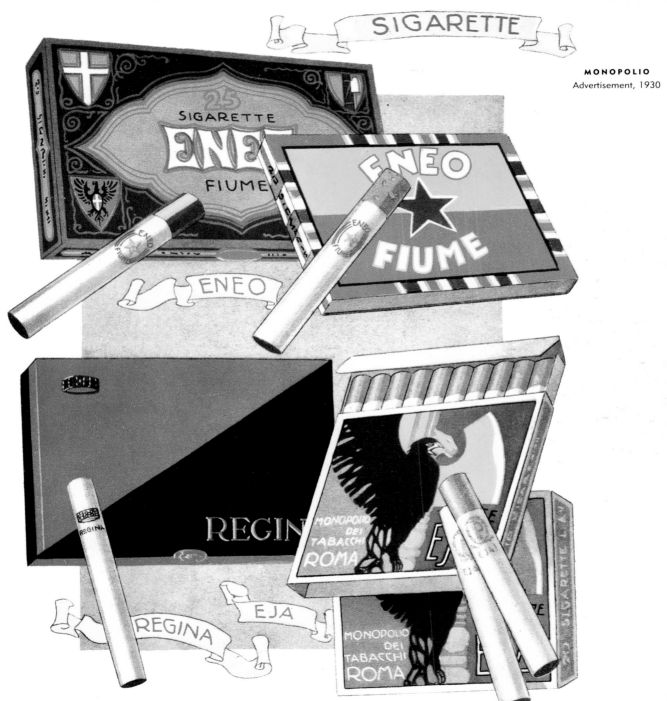

MODIANO
Catalog, 1934

MODIANO
Cigarette package, 1944

SALTO
Cigarette package, 1938

COME UNA SIGARETTA
Sheet music, 1929
Bonfanti

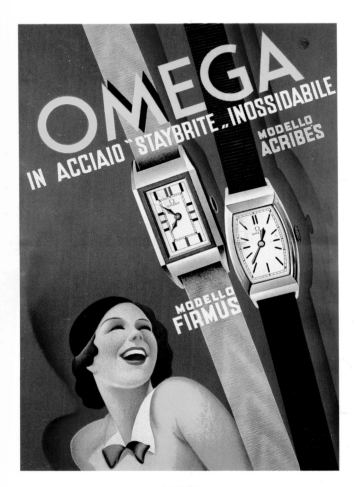

OMEGA
Poster for watches, 1934
Mario Gros

OMEGA
Poster for watches, 1937
Guido Bonacini

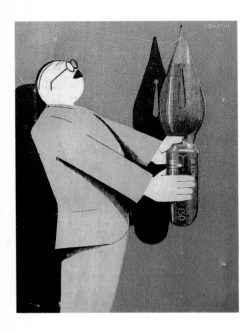

PRESBITERO
Penpoint samples, c.1932
Franco Signorini

QUADRATINO DISEGNATORE
Notebook cover, 1934

DORIS
Pencil package, c. 1937

PRESBITERO
Pencil package, 1938

FILA
Pencil label, 1938

FILA
Pencil package, 1935
D. Tofani

COLORATE FINI

PRESBITERO

PER UFFICIO

FILA

la matita Italiana di qualità

FABBRICA ITALIANA LAPIS AFFINI · FIRENZE

FILA ✳ Copiativo per cucitee ✳ 1033

206 FILA ✳ GRAFITE FINISSIMA ✳ ORION ✳ HB

FILA DISEGNO ★ 205/N°2

FILA COPIATIVO FINISSIMO ✳ TOSCA ✳ 1045

FILA

MATITE POLICROME

D. TOFANI

At the turn of the century advertising posters were responsible for more than half the sales of Italian goods, especially liquor. Wine has always been one of Italy's flourishing industries — as early as 1900 Chianti was exported to virtually every "non-dry" country in the world — and liquor advertisements were the paradigms of publicity. "This explains the numerous beautiful posters," wrote N.G. Fuime in 1926, "which cover one-third of any Italian wall." No other distiller of spirits understood the value of a consistent graphic identity better than Campari, whose graphic designs were created by some of Italy's leading artists. Most extraordinary are the ads, posters, and publications designed in the thirties by Fortunato Depero, whose humorous, cubistic approach represents the most polished use of the Futurist style. Liquor companies were not alone in exploiting appetizing graphics; packages and promotions for Lazzaroni baked goods, Perugina candy, and Buitoni and Motta foods were created by Italy's most respected designers. In a country where meals are rituals, the graphics of food and drink were a feast for the eye.

BUITONI
Poster for pastina, 1927
Federico Seneca

BUITONI
Poster for pastina, c.1932
Federico Seneca

BUITONI
Poster for pastina, c. 1934
Federico Seneca

ALA
Baking powder label, 1934

RIVALDO ROSSI
Wheat label, 1944

STELLA D'ITALIA
Cheese label, 1924

MORANDI
Rice label, 1944

ORZO IDROLITICO
Cereal label, 1940

CANARRI
Fruit label, 1938

CULTU FERTILIOR
Grain label, 1924

VILCO
Meat label, 1946

VIGANÒ
Pasta label, 1945

SIK
Cheese label, 1939

IMPERIALE
Biscuit label, 1932

LAZZARONI
Biscuit display, c. 1930

BARATTI & MILANO
Candy label, c. 1938

LAZZARONI
Biscuit label, 1924

PANETTONE ALEMAGNA
Cake label, c. 1930

MOTTA PANETTONI
Package, 1930

(Overleaf)
PASTICCERIA PAZZAGLIA

PASTICCERIA C. CAFLISCH
Wrapping papers, c. 1935

DOMENICO BRISTOT
Coffee label, 1934

CACAO DI ATTILIO LATTES
Cacao label, 1934

BOTTEGA DEL CAFFE
Coffe label, 1930

CAFFE MOKARABIA
Cup, c.1938

APERITIVO ZAFFERANO
Label, c. 1930
Erberto Carboni

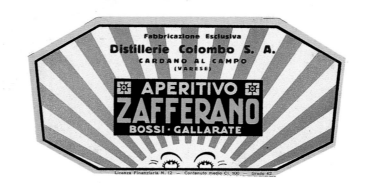

ARANCIO
Juice label, 1932

FRANZINI ARANCIATA
Soda label, 1935

GIGLIO
Advertising fan, c. 1935
E. Caroli

ISOLABELLA
Syrup label, c. 1935

ACQUAVITE
Label, 1936

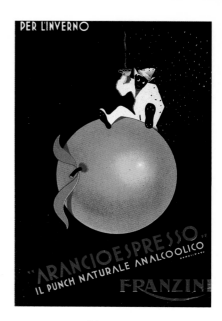

FRANZINI
Soda label, 1935

PARTENOPE
Poster for beer, 1927
Maga (Magagnoli)

MASERA
Advertisement for liquor, 1932

RAMAZZOTTI
Advertisement for liquor, 1930

MIRAFIORE
Advertisement for wine, 1926
Atla

CAMPARI
Various logos, 1920s-30s
Nicolaj Diugheroff

CAMPARI SODA
Ceramic ashtray, c. 1930
Nicolaj Diugheroff

CAMPARI L'APERITIVO
Poster, c. 1931
Marcello Nizzoli

CORDIAL CAMPARI
Poster, c.1931
Marcello Nizzoli

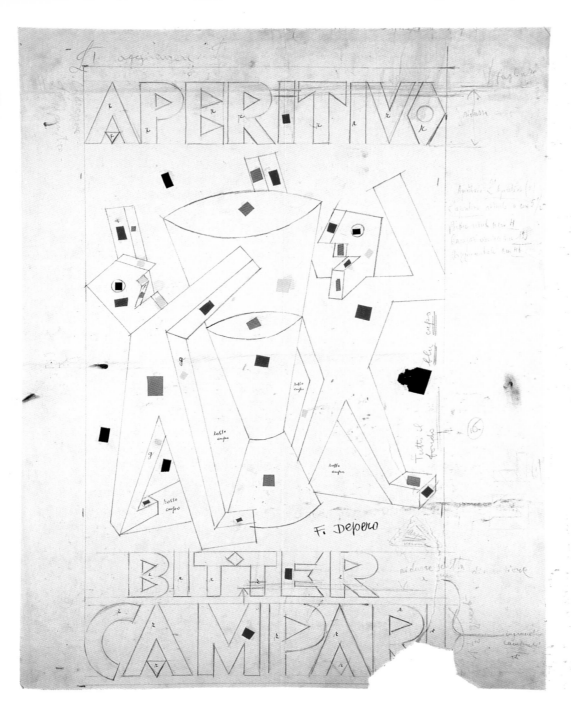

CAMPARI
Concession booth, 1929

**APERITIVO BITTER
CAMPARI**
Sketch, 1927
Fortunato Depero

CAMPARI BITTER CORDIAL
Advertisement, 1928
Fortunato Depero

CAMPARI L'APERITIVO
Advertisement, c. 1930
Fortunato Depero

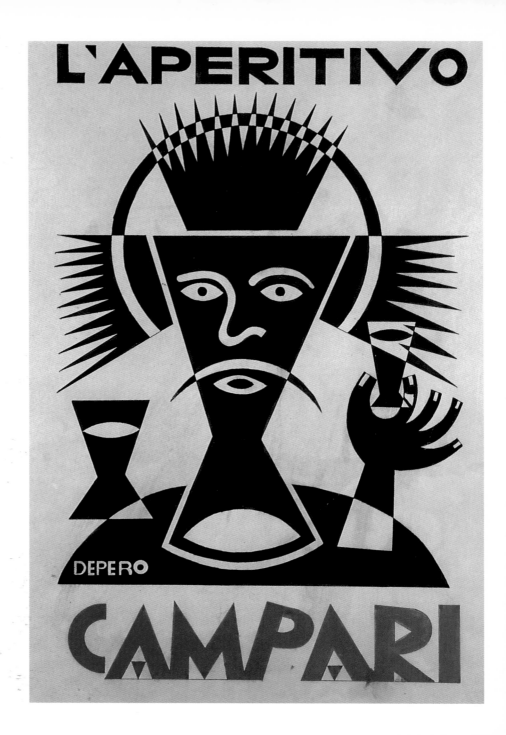

CAMPARI L'APERITIVO
Advertisement, c.1930
after Nizzoli

CAMPARI CORDIAL
Poster, c.1930
Nicolaj Diulgheroff

CAMPARI
Delivery truck, c. 1928

PERUGINA
Poster for chocolates, 1928
Federico Seneca

PERUGINA
Poster for chocolates, c.1929
Federico Seneca

PERUGINA
Poster for chocolates, 1927
Federico Seneca

PERUGINA CHOCOLATES
Label, c. 1928

ALI D'ITALIA
Advertisements for chocolates, 1931
Mario Gros

Italy is famous for its motor cars. Firms like Alfa Romeo, Lancia, Bugatti, and Fiat made the machines on which automotive legends were built. "The motor car industry, its affinities and accessories, has always been of great interest to Italians," wrote N.G. Fiumi in 1926 about the extraordinary number of posters produced at that time. In their reverence for speed the Futurists imbued the automobile with the power of a religious icon, devoting poems, paintings, and graphics to it. After liquor no other advertisements for industry were as ubiquitous, and no other manufacturer was as prolific with its advertising as Fiat. During the twenties Fiat was the largest automotive firm in Europe, and the first to open a special advertising department. Racing added to the allure of the automobile, and posters that idealized this test of man and machine were commonplace. The airplane was also a symbol of futuristic wonder. It is not surprising that Mussolini's own obsession with flying influenced graphics. These depictions were in turn used in ads for the travel and tourist industries, among Italy's most lucrative businesses.

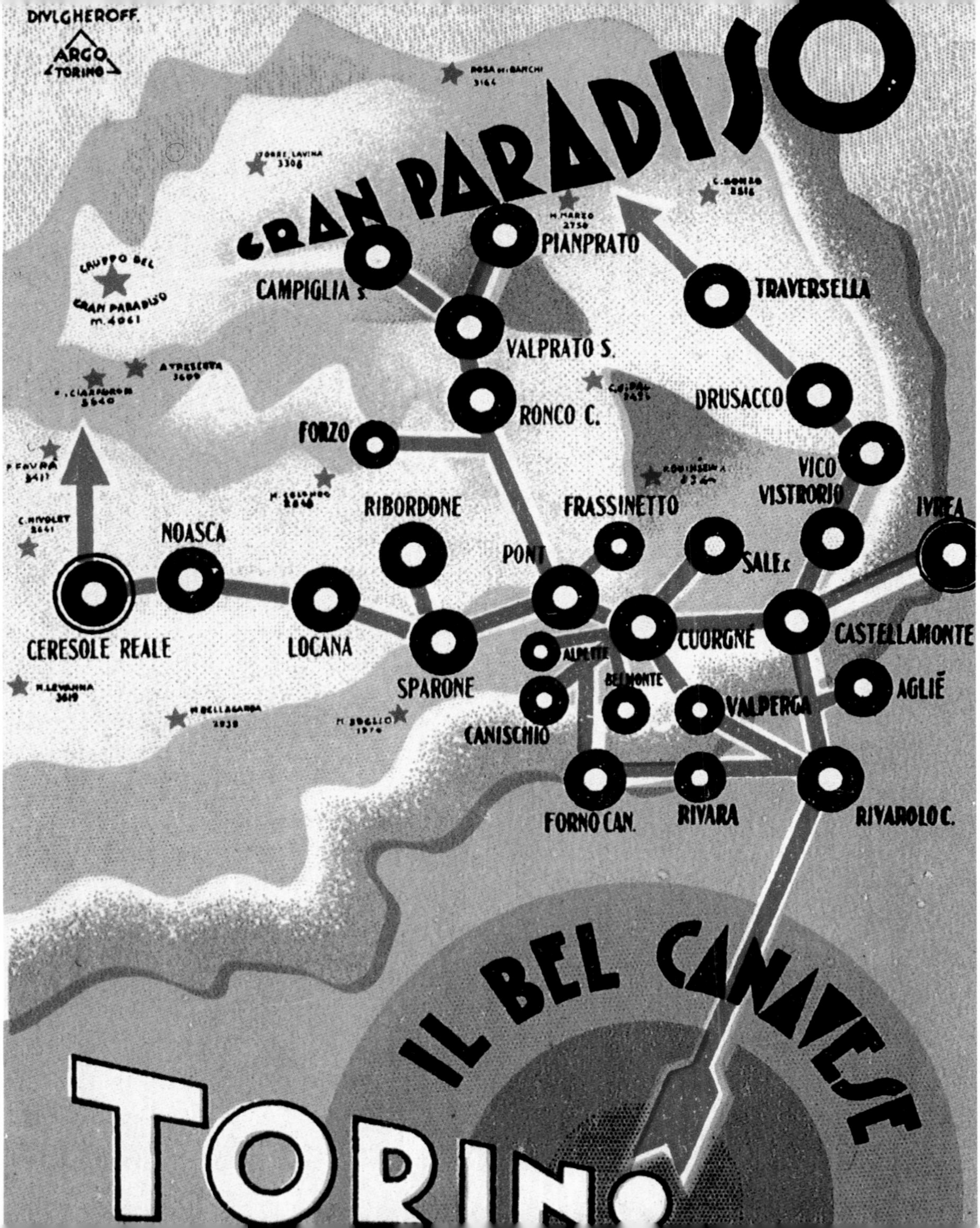

GRAN PARADISO
Travel poster, 1930
Nicolaj Diugheroff

CROCIERA AEREA
DEL DECENNALE 1933
Poster for exposition, 1933
Luigi Martinati

CROCIERA AEREA
DEL DECENNALE 1933
Poster for exposition, 1933
Luigi Martinati

ALI D'ITALIA
Almanac cover, 1930
Bruno Munari

FIERA
Postcard, c. 1926

GIRO AEREO D'ITALIA
Magazine title panel, 1930

**I PERIODICI
DELL'AVIAZIONE ITALIANA**
Advertisement, 1935

**CROCIERA AEREA DEL DECENNALE
1933**
Poster stamp for exposition, 1933
Luigi Martinati

L'ALA ITALIANA
Bookcover, 1939
Yambo

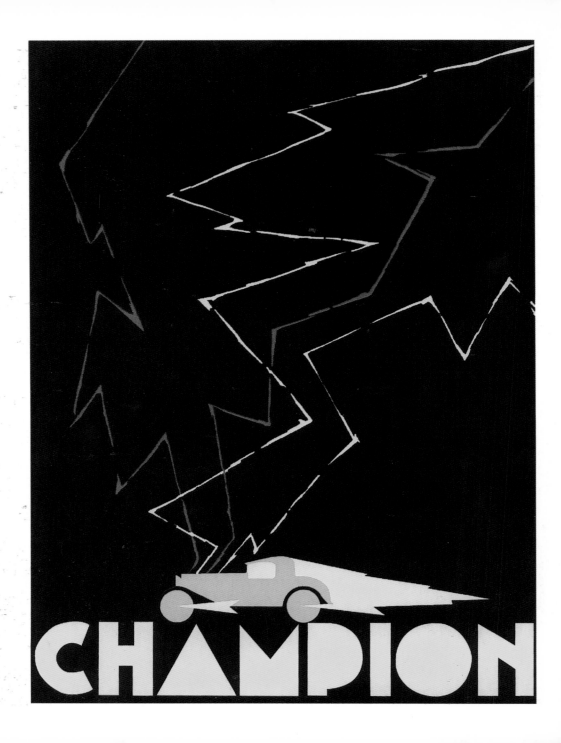

LAMPO
Poster, 1930
Marcello Nizzoli

MAG SPINTER SPARKPLUGS
Poster, 1929
Mario Sironi

SOCIETÀ ANOMINA PNEUMATICI
Logo, 1941

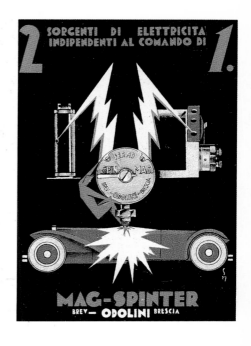

**VIII CAMPIONATO PROVINCIALE
AUTOMOBILISTICO**
Poster, 1930
Erberto Carboni

**IV CUNEO COLLE
DELLA MADDALENA**
Poster, 1930
Lucio Venna

AUTOSERVIZI LAZZI
Advertising fan, c. 1937

BIENNALE DI VENEZIA
Poster for exposition, 1936
Franco Signorini

ESTATE LIVORNESE
Travel poster, 1936

ITALIA
Magazine cover, 1938

BOLOGNA
Travel guide cover, 1932

ITALIA
Magazine cover, 1935

NAPLES
Travel guide cover, 1932

The Futurist rejection of the classical typographic canon disrupted "old snobbish aesthetic ideals." Their use of many discordant typefaces on the same page, an approach referred to as *Words in Freedom*, ignored entirely any semblance of symmetry. These raucous type designs were akin to comic book lettering, but the origin of the sharp-edged, block sans serif frequently used in Futurist book and magazine design is not clear. The artists who promoted it found hand-drawn letters to be well suited to the improvisational nature of their work — more expressive and freer than conventional types. Yet even when texts were set in preexisting type, the faces were often smashed, distorted, and otherwise deformed to emphasize the transient quality of Futurist poetry. Though typographic standards were routinely challenged, typography in Italy, the birthplace of modern type, was still a serious art. Futurism may have influenced many of the era's designers, but others, conforming to the spirit of Italianismo, continued to use nineteenth-century scripts and shadowed letters for contemporary logos.

SOCIETÀ ANONIMA ITALIANA DEROSSI
Page from sign catalog, 1932

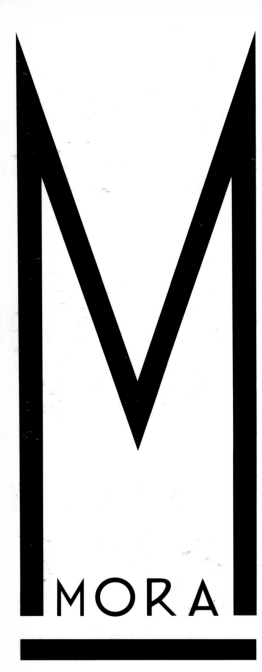

RAPIDA
Typewriter logo, 1931

ZACOSA
Electric company logo, 1943

LINCREO
Building materials logo, 1932

ALBA
Soap label, 1944

ROTOR
Motor company logo, 1934

ALBA
Soap label, 1944

ROTOR
Motor company logo, 1934

DEKROS
Fabric label, 1935

GIVI
Clothes label, 1945

LAVOL
Cosmetics label, 1939

DULCIANA
Chocolate label, 1941

AGIR
Manufacturing company logo, 1938

AEGE
Electronic company logo, 1941

AMBROGIONE
Manufacturing company logo, 1939

VIPLA
Manufacturing company logo, 1940

PRE-FILM
Film company logo, 1941

BOCCANEGRA
Olive oil logo, 1922

FLORANOVA
Perfume logo, 1940

BIOFERO
Pharmaceuticals logo, 1923

ROMANINA
Manufacturing company logo, 1944

DI PI
Electronics logo, 1945

ABBIAMO NUBB

COMMEDIE IN V

di

VOIELLO
Sign for pasta, c. 1938

VASOLITOL

PASTA

Voiello

NAPOLI

VASOLITOL
Cream logo, 1942

NETTO
Cleanser logo, 1930

PRINCIPINO
Chocolate logo, 1937

URIT
Shoe label, 1920

VIAREGGIO
Hotel signs, 1930s

MILANO CONFEZIONI
Advertisement, 1935

AVVISO
Advertisement for Lazzaroni biscuits,
c. 1930

ACQUA RAPIDA
Label for shaving lotion, c. 1930

CARTE DA GIUOCO
Advertisement for cigarettes, 1930

LAMPO
Letterhead for telegram, 1929

NIVO
Tape label, c. 1933

LINTER
Clothes label, 1934

linter

ALDJ
Perfume package, 1944

aldj

eclett

FUTURUM
Machine company logo, 1934

LITTORIA
Film company logo, 1933

littoria FILM

AQUILA
Cement company logo, 1940

SUGORO
Condiments logo, 1936

ECLETTICA
Column head for *Gran Bazar*, 1930
Lucio Venna

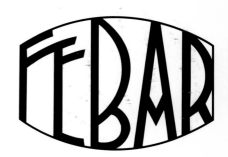

FEBAR
Fabric label, 1932

INCA
Coffee label, 1930

LOMBARDO
Advertisement for cream, 1934

COMPLETO PER 6

su ORDINAZIONE

su Ordinazione

Arrivi

dalle 13 alle 15

RECLAME

INSEGNE
Signs for shop window display, 1930s

VISIBILE · ECONOMICO · RAPIDO · ORDINATO

VERO

VERO
Electric company logo, 1928

ELETTROCONVETTORE

ARIEL

ARIEL
Electric company logo, 1937

M M M MILANO

MMM
Fabric logo, 1937

AVTARCASSA

AUTARCASSA
Logo, 1938

SPIGA
Fashion label, 1944

TESTA ROSSA
Wine label, 1930

CARLI
Olive oil label, 1940

VALENTE
Phonograph company logo, 1939

**GRANDI EMPORI
ALIMENTARI**
Store logo, 1944

MIELUS
Bread label, 1939

AMARETTI DI SARONNO
Poster for biscuits, 1932
Marchesi

Arbasino, Alberto, and Gianni Bulgari. *Cinquanta Anni di Immagini della Più Importante Industria Italiana*, Edizioni di Autocritica, 1984.

Cesarani, Gian Paolo. "Slogans in Statues." *FMR No. 5* (October 1984), Franco Maria Ricci, Milan, 1984.

Commercial Art (Volume II). The Studio, London. 1927.

Fanelli, Giovanni, and Ezio Godoli. *Il Futurismo e la Grafica*. Edizioni Comunità, Milan, 1988.

Hulten, Pontus. *Futurism & Futurisms*, Abbeville Press, New York, 1986.

Lista, Giovanni. *L'Art Postal Futuriste*, Editions Jean-Michel Place, Paris, 1985.

Lista, Giovanni. *Le Livre Futuriste: de la libération du mot au poem tactile*, Editions Panini, Milan, 1984.

Priarone, Giuseppe. *Grafica Pubblicitaria In Italia Negli Anni Trenta*, Cantini, Florence, 1989.

Salaris, Claudia. *Il Futurismo e la Pubblicità: dalla pubblicità dell'arte all'arte della pubblicità*, Lupetti & Co. Editore, Milan, 1986.

Scudiero, Maurizio. *Depero Futurista e l'arte pubblicitaria*, Galleria Fonte D'Abisso Edizioni, Modena, 1988.

Silva, Umberto. *Ideologia e arte del Fascismo*, Mazzotta, Milan, 1973.

Studio Campari Art in Communication: Fortunato Depero. Davide Campari, Milan, 1989.

Vergani, Guido. *Thirty Years and a Century of the Campari Company* (Vol III), Campari, Milan, 1990.

Villani, Dino. *La Pubblicità e i Suoi Segreti*, Editoriale Domus, 1950.

Waibl, Heinz. *The Roots of Italian Visual Communication*, Centro di Cultura Grafica, Como, 1988.